Fetch Your Mother's Heart

lisa luxx

Out-Spoken Press
London

Published by Out-Spoken Press,
Unit 39, Containerville
1 Emma Street
London, E2 9FP

A CIP record for this title is available from the British Library.

First edition published 2021
ISBN: 978-1-8380211-7-7

Typeset in Adobe Caslon
Design by Patricia Ferguson
Printed and bound by Print Resources

Out-Spoken Press is supported using public funding by the National Lottery through Arts Council England and a grant from the Inclusive Indies Fund administered by Spread the Word.

Fetch Your Mother's Heart

for my friends
& for our Cheryl Constance

I sounded like a fire for no reason

—Ocean Vuong

what you lack and the punishment for your lacking are the same

—Kaveh Akbar

longing is the absent chatting with the absent

—Mahmoud Darwish

Contents

chapter IV

chapter V

chapter VI

introduction

It was the four weeks of October, when violence came to me like a firefly illuminating semi-circles of skin. Tender flapping wings of barely there, glowing against the back of my hand where my veins make the shape of a divided love heart.

(1) The October of Cheryl's suicide. Our warmest sister of the sisterHudd, who I met carrying a teapot across an open field as we followed a lady in black cloth to a banquet. Cheryl who always had magic stones in her bosom and placed them in my palm when I was sick with ego, how the milk of her smile settled my scowl. Our warmest sister, who took all her hugs, and with arms crossed threw herself into the afterlife. When I found out, in my home in Beirut, the woman I was in love with held my champagne and held my head. **(2)** Days later, while I was still grieving in Batroun, the woman I was in love with would take our anniversary trip alone, and wrap her body around a tourist, fidelity splitting like chapped skin. I'd forgive her with my loneliness, an outstretched finger asking to be clasped. **(3)** The following Monday we'd drive north to buy a car from my dear elder friends. A car that signified new beginnings. We never got to view the car since their son arrived possessed by desperation for his mother's attention, and attempted to murder his father right there in the living room. Only when someone much taller than you is summoning blood will you learn the extent of your loyalty. I got everyone to safety, but with muscles tired from running for our lives, I remained terrorised by how much I recognised his hunger. **(4)** By now the gas stations were full of brawling, as scarcity sizzled and sank normalcy into drains and broken concrete. On that eternal Thursday, while drinking arak with Samsam, we got a call telling us to meet now in the streets downtown. We arrived to flares, riots, small fires everywhere, mopeds growling in packs. The revolution had erupted.

Our imagination persists beyond our limitations and so our longing will always be a type of grief. While the leaders of our father-cultures force citizens into starvation, I watch us thrash in our beds, in our streets, in our godlands, for we cannot remember where we hid our great mother's heart, and we need it.

How soft I became after those four weeks. How fright became foreplay. How violence begets tenderness, how tenderness begets violence. How there was no bargain left, only oscillation between extremes and I said *brutal, brutal, keep me close, for it is here where the firefly glows, it is here where the wings of nothing make the most natural light undulate, undulate over this broken heart I wear beneath my knuckles.*

And then, I began this book.

lisa luxx
January 2021

chapter I

to write the wrongs of centuries, we must brew our own tools

no physician predicted this

between major and minor notes

an itch of a bird song
& you, my dawn

grinding saffron

year ٢١٠
pestle & mortar

bury in me your sigh
as our soil carries dead
in airless secrets

i hold your breath

centuries persist
men dumb & ink

my saffron grind crushes
beard & bible
to dust

all of this, embroidered in waistbands
ya zarrifa *how I dress you up*

petrified in gold thread
sewn by mist

we survive the long hush

i hold your breath

drench   tonight's bedsheets in sweat

wet, tip, & reaching
we open   lips

exhale   saffron ink
your cupped hand, gathering

they call this *lesbian*

I kiss your knee   call you *comrade*
we laugh & the sound is a language that
hasn't been written yet

majnouneh

& here we are
eating pistachios & watching
the earth become a mountain
in order   to kiss one star

I crossed a continent to tell you
about Qays   this is how my salt enters you

the sun devours everything
but as it falls we *wow, wow*
at all it gives, all wow light
orange sublime falling
reflected in your face

when mist conceals its view
you need to know I will still   mountain

even wandering its peaks
I cannot measure
how high this mountain rose
nor how orange
falling   always renews

I will always   mountain   you.

You ask if mountains can fall, I say *sand dune.*

You ask what happened to Qays
I dust salt off your lips

& admit:

he was found alone, killed,
beside a   sand dune
gazelle lapping at the salt salt
blood from his wound.

softness brings you to worlds within the immediate

'there is no distance in childhood … whatever is absent is impossible, irretrievable, unreachable.'

— Rebecca Solnit

We are barefoot as new beginnings
washing each other warm, under an outpour
she rubs the soap bar under my fingernails

suds rolling down her ribs.

When she finishes I stare at my palms, every
wrinkle & crease, the weight of everything
held written in the language of skin

this autobiography of wanting.

(In the village a newborn sees her hands
for the first time: marvellous & grotesque
a pair of oceans on the ends of her arms.)

I step out amid steam, embalmed in heat,
piggy-back my Layla to her bed our mouths
smell like caramel. I hold the moment.

Another crease in my palm.

Press my skin to your ear now to hear a song
being sung somewhere very far away:
someone we stopped searching for
is calling out
for shore

i was sleeping while she was letting him inside

i dream of mum crying

at the dinner table   while my sister watches

Snapchat   a mound of salt where i usually sit

i dream of Layla pregnant by a man named Steve

or Tony   not me   i bump into them in Ashrafieh

him grunting   me panting   her glowing

i dream of a high school boy   who tried to plug

his stretched earlobe with a huge fake diamond stud

after his mum said emo wasn't man enough

after scooter license hand-job in the top field i told

him *sure diamond studs are super manly*

i dream i'm sleeping   i dream of

loving her so good   that when i am within her

fallen flowerheads rise   my blue sky   leaving

her pregnant with our child

romance in action #17
***aka* we need to talk about the dominance of desire**

you know our souls are small gods in the underworld
tethered like shadows to our love

A Good Man acts like sunlight
offering forgiveness in cartons of orange juice

if he tells you he's a Noah   throw the white
light of Alma all around
or whatsapp your local hoodwitch

trust me, I called myself good once
while my fingers were tangled
in her nine strings

but I'm not here to tell you what to do
just to listen

boys with stallions in their chests
aren't stable

we all want to be wanted until we find ourselves
pouring salt out our bodies
& pretending to be extinct

A Good Man acts like sunlight

stretching darkness as he falls

after the day's divide   you're swaying down the
long street   you don't see a foot clamp down   on the
edge of your shadow   you keep on swaying
breeze ~~bitch~~ breeze

I come from a country of misfired apologies
where smoking is a sin & wishes
are weapons that leave no evidence

your shadow squirms under his foot   tucks it
in his pocket   keeps one finger rubbing on its edge
it's still there

only you know if your voice at
climax is your soul's attempt to tunnel
through the dampness & enter the big gods'
overworld   once & for all

A Good Man sirens home   hot tap   burns germs off
his hands & sleeps   your shadow
pulled taut   bound to his rise

but this is my book, not his

modifying the sahara

we march forward towards the shore of light
bewildered by one another's
addictions unarmoured & aging
chasing something
so weightless
we'll never know
when we have it
the leather of our shoes wore thin ancestors ago

calf cramp we march

I hope the giants start praying soon but they're too
busy running their fingers through desert

while I go after everything that tumbles from their hands
thinking it's for me

if any of us reach where we're heading it means
we're too late

chapter II

it's only called a 'revolution' when we feel proud of what happened today *aka* worry when they start to call it 'the situation'

& there I go > riding down main roads wrong way > to reach the neighbourhood where my mates > are pouring small cups of ahwey > & tightening straps on their gas masks > each orders her Careem's free ride > to the women's frontline > chanting peace between warring sons

feet soles blacken from tar breaking into our homes > burning tyre roadblocks > will be replaced with plant pots > & wind carries chants west > *thawra!* > rain beats on earth's chest > *thawra!* > a neighbour is humming under her breath *hala hala hala ho…* >>

church bells thunder as people without raincoats & people with raincoats > disrupt highways banging pots & pans > empty water containers make good drums > harmonicas > singing bowls > triangles > kazoos > o the nutseller is climbing street signs > corn man sells-out every day > dawn gave birth in martyr's sq > breastmilk pouring everywhere > > >

we live like this a while. petting the uneasy silence below it all. as Kalashnikovs rest on the bodies of their men.

definitions of hunger

silence /ˈsʌɪləns/ noun
the opposite of eating

eat /iːt/ verb
the act of singing

handprint /ˈhandprɪnt/ noun
what happens after silence

some feminists came painted   old
Silence's handprint across their mouth

a mother-age stranger thumbs up
my banner   *no is a complete sentence!* ha

rubbing my back now   we walk side by side
no words exchange we face up   tide fighting sky

chants I pronounce wrong I meant right
moon couldn't sleep   hung belly full at 3.33

we're dancing laughing clapping ha dancing when
man beside me pours gasoline on himself

& eats —

trailed home silence
from the ashes of shins
kettle boiled 3 times
forgot to brew tea   ha

    prepared ramen
    with handprints
    still clinging to me

can there be such a thing as extreme tenderness?

III - now
Look at us, blinking.
A candle is consuming itself with desire
flame light wailing across Layla's skin,

window open to the sky.
& no, it isn't a full moon yet,
it's the crescent laughing type.

IV - still
The laughing type.

V - before
Celestial bodies trying to stifle their cry,
laughter after adrenaline subsides.

At the attempted murder scene
I am trying not to smile

into thick mountain night
as my phone covered in blood
dials the police line

we wait for four men in fatigues
to arrive in a pick-up truck
guns strapped to their hips

where men carry weapons women carry kids.

VI – now
Crickets scratch the night as Miriam pours flower
tea & sends good prayers to the asylum. Down
the mountain, Layla & I are just breath & skin hairs
brushing; fingers running through long grass:
tenderness: a body's way of forgiving violence.

VII - before
Miriam clings to the door as we run for our lives
never turning our backs all at once in case
longing — still bloodthirsty & crazed — catches
up. Flies chase the miracle hobbling
beside me. Somewhere behind:
Miriam's voice an ice cream van chime.

As her son is taken to jail, she tells a tale
her mother told her as a young girl
of a mother whose son
hungered for her love so much,
he cut her heart out of her chest,
but running away he slipped & fell

his mother's blood reached out
like two apron strings
tying a stairway to heaven
only her son would ascend.

come march of mothers

ore mother mined in mountain
labour mother mined in milk
        wheat mother mined
        air mother mined
        care of mother mined
        looted

mother tongue / mother spirit / root & bloom

there is no revolution until a runaway
of maddening mothers
abandon England
playing wooden flutes
& we children follow
possessed (or starving)

the cartesian body: a coupling

And although possibly (or rather certainly, as I shall
say in a moment)

i've nothing to seem or say that isn't in breast
or bone

I possess a body with which I am very intimately
conjoined,

and i possess a million bodies from which my
ancestors were dethroned

yet because, on the one side, I have a clear and
distinct idea of myself

and on the other side is white man's clear and distinct
idea of myself

inasmuch as I am only a thinking and unextended
thing, and as, on the other,

he himself of all his sins crowned himself the soul, making
body from Black folk, indigenous and women.

I possess a distinct idea of body, inasmuch as it is
only an extended and unthinking thing,

he broke the link between soul and body, de-godified
our skin. here in the hierarchy we live

it is certain that this I [that is to say, my soul by which
I am what I am],

belongs to the empire of man and

is entirely and absolutely distinct from my body, and can
exist without it.

Can we body-people, distinct from his reason, come to
exist without it?

dinner during the week of rage

Sunflower oil sizzles beneath potatoes
and cauliflower in the frying pan.
Tariq's eating warak einab standing up
gas mask round his neck and goggles
strapped above his forehead.
Water hits the fresh coriander
between my fingers, pinning each
small petal down against my flesh
and you giggle about the lasers
you picked up to shine in the eyes
of the darak when they come to beat
us up again.

Mischievous, I say. You limp to
the lemon, rubber bullet wound
in the back bend of your knee.
Tahini over each dish, salt, hamoud
Tariq pours sugar in his snayniyeh &
we each damn *fuck this government*
in turn and the oil has dried up
the garlic is cooked. I say, *let's eat*
and I'll follow you
to martyr's square.

I get the words for 'lemon' and
'will die' mixed up. *Hamoud.*
Ha mout. You squeeze in a little
more. As if I didn't add enough.
The halloum crisped to crunch.
A will die pip lands on your plate.
Sahteyn.

how it tastes to arrive from very far away: a broken ghazal

it wouldn't be wild to start to wonder:
was it all for onion?
what else tells the safe body to grieve,
but the sunder of onion?

when she begged the soul up my windpipe,
it was the closest I got
to home, we shared shankleesh as teargas roamed
her breath sung of onion.

you, running away from the table, listen
when you hear *eat more*
it means belong here, it means *be long* here.
a tumble of onions

soldier to where your body yearns to stay.
a moped commotion
passes down below. on window ledge an angel
juggling onion

laughs through chattering teeth. foster kids are
cattle; a hand against
window pane; who was holding my hair back, if
I chundered onion?

instead of saying I like your smile, you say *your*
bones are showing.
samsam swapped a roll up cig — as sound bombs
rumbled — for an onion,

tore off a piece gave it to me. let me tell you
why we're better
off needing: I watched asphyxiating teenage boys
shun onions

& throw burning canisters back at police,
bare hands unbothered.
we learn freedom by following echoes of chains
drumming. onion

tells the safe body to grieve, before we eat,
mouth full with empty.
little lise, do you realise yet why *I love you*
hums like onion?

chapter III

running etcetera

I hold my breath and run, run down roads while mamas and tetas clutch dressing gowns closed and bolt shutters. *This kind of wind carries disease!* Is shouted from a balcon above. I close my nose with a hard pinch and I run down the road. A light is on in the boxing gym, one punching bag swings alone. I run and run and run down the road. Still I am not home. Nose pinched shut, mouth vice tight, dimpled. I run and run and run down the roads. Wind ferocious, rattles the neon cross, church door is bolted, locked. *Does the wind not want to rest, does the wind not want to rest with me!* I run and run, lungs swollen as hot feet in leather binds. *Will the wind not just drop this dust! Just let it go!* I yell to the airborne itch that roams. I run and run. And still I am not home. Eyelashes hash across each iris, lids half close. Pinch tighter nose. Still I am not home. *Doesn't the wind just want a cup of tea? Please!* I choke, but still I am not home. And I run (x3), and still (x2) I'm not. I,   and
still. I am no—   not

'home'

a hushed séance on the tongue.
  which way do I cast this spell?

circles

'if we're not writing poems for our friends, then what are we doing writing?'

—Safia Elhillo

my passport says I was born in
    a muscle of women

    who smell like sage & sawdust

    in our culture we pay rent
    in the amount of times we say *babe*

    there's Jadey Jade planting sunflowers
outside my door
    so when I open up it's always noon

whenever I pull out my own teeth Yasmine shares
    her smile between us

& we chant gossip to call in our dead, ancestors
    clicking tongues
                every voicenote a spell
    (swearing incantations so our countries may
    stop terrorising themselves
    so our minds may stop terrorising
    themselves)

good witches don't dream, they design:
Dayna's pencil marks on wood build our ark
Tazzy carves spoons
    no one ever said *I'm lost*
    while serving soup

o goddess! let us be bad bitches forever
these babes, these myths, imagine the ancestors they
become

We gap folk, who didn't just sing for our supper
bowl

who made the bowl birthed every throat
muse & master

of every song

I don't need a home

I got sisterhood

Arms gather me in while I wash our names

& wait for lovers to come through big enough to
temple these daughters

honey, lute, praying, dew

earned

My sisters have been through it

My women are countries, my people hold
rivers run gold, streams of house keys, we pass
between o

my sisters are wild & keen, on shivering
globe

We are one stateless nation of

yes bitch I know you!

They say *luxxy* or *lise* when they mirror mirror

or silence silence as we watch each
other eat

taking it in turns
to savour a bite,

spit it out,

pass it on,

my feast is your feast, your hunger cadavers me

the alive is where we bury our dead

when a sis gives her body back to Mother
her heartbeat becomes a tide to the ocean
I bathe there offering fried fish to the water

Let her ghost rise at my window while I sleep
Let the train come while a woman weeping
under a streetlamp holds her raincloud on a ribbon

Let helium dangle its feet beneath laughter
as I pop corks towards the sky shouting
A breakdown is a breakthrough!
O stars you sweethearts for shooting

If Cheryl would come back holding a teapot
I would follow her towards the feast again
Let me dance five rhythms as a funeral march
Have you seen what sorry looks like

after its third bottle of water?
The trains are coming. Alight
at the edge of the harvest

There's my hometown in the tuna can
& death is a small boy riding his pony
of bones behind the train carriage

We turn our eyes away from each other
as skydivers' hands unclasp & promise eternity
promise eternity promise eternity promise
to give these sinews as jewels for her ghost

pulling myself together

I held a corn stick   watching   my city
in terror,   ablaze.   Shouted with
everyone   else   dancing.   Left
to return to my flag,   which was humming,
fluffing   country.   Ate chips & spoke of
albe   a playing card   I'd left behind.

My foster home was my first
connecting flight waiting
room kid suitcase
of questions, that's
language hungering.

My hands are searching for each other.
An old woman mirrors my gestures, prayer position:

that's opposites held for mending
I'll pull together and wait for you, god.

I eat my greens   then smoke a cigarette   make love
with a lump in my breast tongue hot in the ear of
madness narrow as the streets busy as dread   I run
in front of a moped clutching my sleeve
exhaust yelling to the afterlife

we're here!
can you
hear us?

and

on the edge of thunder, our mates nosedive into
steak, first meal of the week, ravenous bodies living
on adrenaline and snacks, the revolution a diet
plan

I swallow three beers before you come. before they
leave: strengthened by food, surging home all thawra
backpack and flags to frenzy tender relief. as they
meat

fuck their way through shake and collapse we down
bullets at a street bar and you take my hand, I follow,
up the metal spiral stairway, you search in me as I
watch

us in the mirror and a cleaning man stands outside
our cubicle mopping one spotless spot, and we pass
military tanks on our way home, where I invite
myself

up since you won't and we're too close to the end
now for me to pretend dignity and Australia is on fire
and Yorkshire is in floods and fists are rising
seedlings

punching their way out of muck and I rest, head on
your chest and listen to my tick and throb. I sleep,
beside you, my heart, in the same bed as my body.
when

we wake, the earth has grown sicker, headlines snap
against the window and I smile, kiss you, no need to
leave, hear a friend lost an earlobe and we order
pastries.

as we shrapnel

I'm losing punch hugs & piano skin
losing the family we made
before the scattering

where my thirst kept recycling   or pretending to
stacking fourteen bags of plastic against
night's sky

losing dog rivers   piss never where
we left it

losing the morning of the afternoon   sipping gossip
bitter   from chipped coffee cups

Where's the glue of hashish now?   The peace
lily drowning in her own words?

Each of us   a landmine   stepping on each other's
toes   & loving it

chapter IV

sandcastles in eternal renewal

we march forward
towards that shore of light

c h a

s i n g

a g r a i n

o f

s

a

n

d

on things we can't let go of
aka how long does it take to grow somebody out of you?

8 months ago: blood fingerprints
still on my phone & on my clothes.

define hope? a stale prayer
we hold in our mouths

while pretending to be adults.
on the bed you paint my toes,

a howling outside turns over fruit boxes
searching for its mother's heart.

brush sweeping over nail, nail. you bend in,
use your thumb to wipe paint off my skin.

wax drips from candelabra onto polaroid:
me dancing. define war?

//

8 months later: nail polish
still on. measuring the time it takes

for a touch to leave the body.

there's a thin line of maroon, still clinging
to my left big toe. your voice

echoes on the phone, complains
I'm breastfeeding a bruise.

//

there's a foreigner lost in the underground
much like a *no* moves through my body

much like I pinch the edge of day, softly begging
when the knife of midnight flashes

& all our sons are on their knees

//

drink honey straight from the jar
drink two glasses of water
drink the ink out of my tattoos
drink the saliva from between my teeth
drink the gunshots of a choking boy celebrating
drink the edge of where I left you
drink the Jerusalem out the nation
drink the sweat off my stomach
drink the bodies out the river
drink a glass of prosecco with me just because
someone said *great work today*
                great work today
there's a small god inside you fighting to get out

beyond us are only mothers

fields of fathers stood swaying dumb struck

lifting lint from pockets & throwing fluff towards

the sky open palms & half-closed eyes

a child under three can't stop laughing

swinging arms around & shouting curses

what if you don't have to punish yourself

foster kid # lucky got roast dinner Sundays

Labrador lake walks power ranger play toys

what if you don't look back

every woman who was a generous vine

is with Hades now don't Orpheus

the darkness is a cackling

black & it makes dust of bone she's rivers run

blue is a myth of the eyes far away things

waves skies longing blue was never coming

romance in action #72
aka we need to talk about the urge of desire

with every seed that tunnelled its way up to the light,
with the dust rising at the racing tiger's feet, with the
tiger & the coyote & the tiger & the beat of the sun
cracking mud like it's tearing clothes off the earth's
body, with the last stitch in the dress of a dervish,
with the rising ivy promising itself to eat this
building, eat this building whole, with all the force
that came before, was me begging to be born, all
that rising, howling, stomping, growling, purging,
urging, urging, urging to live, to live — so I could
love, so I could love, so I could love you.*

---

* & yet I am scared to go out in the street lest I see you in it.
I am scared to go out in the street lest I don't see you in it.

what if our hearts rumbled like our stomachs do

o wait —

tipping bolognese onto spaghetti I realise
I forgot to chop onion, fry garlic or cook

soy mince   I masticate with my godlike
capacity to erase   & throw salt over my shoulder

outside the window   laundry swaying on the line
has completely forgotten the shape of my body

a kid picking dandelions
keeps calling them sunflowers

tried to tell you I love you this morning
but my mouth made chainsaw sounds

there are so many ways to be lonely
putting on glass boots & running

over this silence towards you
is by far my least favourite

but this is how I'll learn
too much fire gives birth to nothing

wicker people

Your leaders don't know what you look like when
you're sleeping.

A mother who never got to keep her children
wouldn't know being startled is the closest thing to
being found.

Our neighbourhood uncle hangs plum trees from his
shopfront while a woman stuffed with straw is
ploughing through tomatoes & pickles, sure she left
her love here.

(O is your god laughing?
lol wicker people of eternal underwhelm
all fuse & searching.)

Call me daddy, call me angel, startle me.

> Nevermind. I switch my phone off so I may
> hunger in peace. The blades of my wings
> rest, feathers are bone knives in impeccable
> sheaths.

(O did a keyboard warrior turn our placards
into wall art?)

Outside, a jobless mathematician is counting his own
armhairs & humming loudly over the missiles.

No one sees what happens to the woman
but we all watch the tomatoes & pickles
hit the pavement.

dipping buckets of longing into the well of grief

some people stand at one another's wishing wells with bags of pennies. chucking rust and asking for too much, as if needing this or that isn't soiling the very thing the well could offer. others stand at one another's wishing well, lowering their buckets into long damp endless *no.* o the empty vowel, no is how adults sing the void. most lift their bucket filled with absence, clatter tin against stone *how will I quench the thirst of my flesh, or wash it clean, with all this nothing?* few keep lowering their bucket, aging and unromantic, until they reach a pool rich with lost wishes, & a warning to whoever listens: *news from afar is making its way towards you*

well beneath the
longing-grief is a small
boy   sharing   orange
slices with his sister under
the sun picking off the pith
wafting flies off her fingers
promising to always
protect   her

chapter V

is love, then, metaphor in practice?

gods, let me tell you what I've learnt:
Your son will come to carve himself out of you. This is how he ends you. His name curdling in his mother's mouth.

Layla and I drove up Matn Highway. I fiddled with the broken radio, trying to find the right wire to pinch to make Nao sing. It was 5.21pm.

Now tell me: who did I betray to spend my 29th summer eating peaches? And, do we pour the quality we're most afraid of into others — to give us swing room to attack it?

As Miriam put the zhourat on the table, I told her husband what I'd learnt about my ankles. *The strongest part of my body is the part that oscillates between extremes.*

In the next room, their son, my age, was smelling the last traces of his mother's scent on his skin, and panicking.

There's a lot I was to learn:

- how a mother would use me as a shield against her son's longing
- an attempted murder scene is no different to a murder scene, except the dead can't invite you back for flower tea the following Wednesday
- you can only measure your loyalty when someone taller than you is summoning blood
- no matter how many times I call her Layla she would never call me Qays, only men get to be loved as madmen

I watched a son carving, with a shard of broken glass. He didn't notice his pants fall down: so I learnt, violence is the most vulnerable way to say *my hands have nothing left to hold.* His eyes reminded me of my own.

In glass houses, a thrown stone breeds a thousand daggers. At 11.51pm Layla left me for another man. I learnt togetherness was an army against empty space. And, I could no longer smell her scent upon my skin.

how we halve ourselves

All the sons taking chainsaws to the sea, holding
their mother's hand as the ground beneath pierces the
soles of her feet.
All the sons pissing in the well of longing, chewing
Efes cans to mush & holding their daughters hostage.
All the sons grasping their sons by the waist,
whispering weapons & tasting like liquorice.
All the sons dragged in gangs like pebbles pulled
under the white froth of waves, failing to cling to the
sand that shaped them.
All the sons whose pants fell down in the storm &
who never raised them before throwing punches.
All the sons who painted the world blue before we
knew blue is only the shade of distance.
All the sons mourning themselves.
All the sons taking their chainsaws to the sea, trying
to cap time in clocks, snap eternity, stoppers of their
mother's endless birthing.

//

I take my muzzle off & make promises with my
fingers crossed behind my back.

Stopped spending time with men because I can't bear
how similar we are.

Started boxing where we hold each other's body
parts like roadkill wrapped in a spare jacket.

> Swing round. Temple kick. Sweat bead to
> sweat bead, like we're threading rosaries.

Men get to rip apart their own flesh then send
maggots as love letters but women don't let other
women get away with that.

Spend my adult life trying to get gentle babes to say
easy boy, easy as I *ruff ruff*

I'm not half as Alsatian as I want to be.

We learnt how to enact our desire for women through
the same films the sons all did.

A glove crunches against my rib, this is how we
knock on the door of skin asking to be let in

meat closest to bone is the tenderest.

//

Punches don't land in dreams, I tried. There was a
night Layla held my temper while I slept, so I could
meet him. The son my flesh pretended not to
become. Hair red as my birth mother's. Deplorable,
until he put on knight's armour & promised to listen
to why he mustn't treat women with the sharp end of
his wanting, how it carves the nose off the goddess.
How many dreams will it take to raise him?

i always thought dying was the best way to say i love u but

when the sons did what they did to Beirut

I knew then
that I must stop cupping my father's silence in my
hands & pouring it over my eyes

I'm terrorised by our proximity
said one nation to another

while two women pray with all their nudity
to close the gaps between their bodies

I walk into a warzone
t-shirt still wet from
my father's tears

who watches me return to what he escaped

no matter how far away you run
you must carry the soil of your teta's country
in your shoes

loyalty is never stepping foot on
another land no matter how many
borders you cross nor how many
generations pass

my father is trying to blow kisses as
my plane takes off but the cloth
around his face keeps them captive

rituals keep outliving us   return to them whenever
someone catches you with your shirt buttoned wrong
& a smoke signal rising from your head

the seashells have almost finished howling   & my
uncle is reciting poems with the news on mute

if it feels impossible
it means you're going the right way

I hope my dad knows that I will return
& I will bring him fifty-two cypress seeds
one for every year he couldn't look back

we don't make love we make live

it will be the days no one follows *I died*
with *and was reborn* like they used to

the days when everyone will be drunk
& asking each other for help

it will have been a long while since two
passersby bumped into each other

like flutes on a wind chime knocking
accidental song out of a stranger's body

two girls will be high as concrete
summoning the moon

one will be knackered
from lugging sheet music out of rubble

the other
will be holding up every shard
of glass to the light
looking for a scream
she may or may not have dropped here

with humidity blurring the mountains
air con drip drips

& I will roll
up another one
stomach churning in the heat

these will be the days when bone collectors in
cufflinks order our nations to forget

we will become sudden to remember
one another   you & I
a reunion resisting amnesia

then, I will be holding your small wet pulse
in my open jaw   looking at you like a dog
cradling in his mouth what he's forbidden to chew

two startled creatures in cotton t-shirts
practising being alive

chapter VI

speaking out loud

we learn languages from our mothers
عربي was my father tongue

I watch the ocean
one eye covered by my dad's palm

another day passes where no brilliance
grows inside me

how embarrassing to trail river from your shoe
while walking through concrete

my throat won't fit around my ancestors

for 28 years I was wearing the features
of a man I didn't know
          my face a missing poster

tell me how this body felt home explode
on the edge of Damascus
while I was in bed in Yorkshire
          this half-carved monument
          is where geography stops pretending

//

what if there were no languages
just empty mouths and full ones
                    dancing or silence

when Layla wore her hair down it meant she was
excited to see me

sniffing is the nose asking questions

if I dream of running it means someone inside me
still believes in the future

a cliff speaks in two directions
eroding & expanding

my body speaks to me in desert

to foreigners
it speaks pollen

counting was invented so we knew when to meet
& when to panic
I count myself in sand

rain taps secrets against earth's skin

coffee speaks fortune in sediment, grief
does the same

no one can hear each other but they're all still talking
I listen to them aiming mindlessly around one
another's silhouettes each person holding their
symbols to their chest

//

I bathe in a woman who has the same name my
father wanted to give me she tastes like
everything I'm not; we both translate as light
yet we speak like worms rubbing through the
territory
of one another's underearth by mistake

my friends change their names often
& our mouths mutate
it's how we sing *i'm a shape-shifting bitch*
you don't know who you lovin'

our names reply *you're a wild eternal honey*
& i got you

in the language of queer names are deities
that walk ahead of our bodies

//

I elongate the vowels in your name to hold you in my mouth a moment longer we bend Fridays until they snap & I'm pushing my rings back on fingers covered in you after spending the night washing myself sacred in your fountain our bodies speak a language our minds are yet to learn text me like you hold me impossible

in batroun

Sat with our fingers in a carcass and the sun on our backs, I said *it's here, between these two rocks that I feasted with the ghost of my suicide friend, and it's here that I made love to a Layla I worshipped, as seagulls and men threw candy in the air.*

He asked, *then doesn't this place make you sad?*

I didn't answer for I was mesmerised by the meat replenishing itself on the bones, and the sun too, would soon drown in its own beauty   behind us

for a subculture to resist capitalist co-opting it must remain impossible to define

Dyke is not my sexuality* dyke is my gender: the She that exists outside the male gaze. The earth is a dyke, if you held her in bed you'd sink into the softness of her skin and she'd flex her bicep in response, knowing gold you are forbidden to mine for. Dyke is my political party, I've seen a city in rubble and watched butches and femmes knot hairs and carry whole neighbourhoods beneath the paving stones while gay boys bowed and made their speeches. Dyke is my street fighter of choice, the way I square my shoulders when I mean 'listen', dyke is the way I listen. Dyke is how I accessorise with bite marks but would marry the cradle. Dyke is the splinters and snags in my fingers from chopping wood, dyke is how I'll always keep you warm. There is a religion to dyke, a belief in the bond and bind in the women and non-binary kind who choir eternal and pulse in formation. Dyke is every no we spell with possibility, every rapture made with mouth shields and dew. Dyke the lucky strike, dyke the uncontainable, dyke the symbol that fails in order to succeed. They invented guns when they couldn't catch birds, dyke is still the ungrabbable wing. Dyke is both my nerves and my steel, dyke moon in water, dyke sun chiselling clouds to let tension out. I learnt to hold my breath, which trained me to submarine into the deepest bonds where we pass in-jokes and lightning bolts between us. Dyke the comrade, dyke the harvest, guardian o friend! Among bike chains and clippers, horoscopes and crystals, with the blessed and the butch, my god we feel true. Come now, every, b-o-i, stud, bad bitch and honey,   you are a horizon.

---

* My sexuality is Men Don't Deserve Me.

questions for the front and back of time

Every day I have to come to ask myself: am I acting in a way that is worthy of my ancestors and am I a worthy ancestor? So that should I cease in the crossfire of living, I shall know I was born, brewed and potent. I shall know I did nothing but hot iron purpose: sunlight. That is, if the baton passes hands with few fouls and good grace, may I be your ancestor. Young fire, spark dreaming of the flame; may I be your ancestor as the wood was mine, as the tree hung dry, dying, so that the smoke may one day speak symbols into a clear night.

modifying the sahara
aka sandcastles in eternal renewal

Everything that falls in orange keeps
searching through its afterlife until it lives again,

infinity running through its outstretched fingers:
leaves, fruit, setting sun

a journey is not made up of the cities a traveller
drinks wine & swaps coins in
but of the empty space between each

bless us, chasing grains of sand

the sky above Beirut splits into seven
& we glimpse the big gods
pouring salt on graph paper
& watching us

with our fingers outstretched
& our voices more ancient
than our bodies

notes and glossary

to write the wrongs of centuries, we must brew our own tools

Thank you Selma Dabbagh and Saqi Books for commissioning this poem and first publishing it in *We Wrote In Symbols: Lust and Erotica by Arab Women.*

The poem was developed in reference to research and translations by Sahar Amer, Pernilla Myrne, and Samar Habib.

majnouneh

Majnouneh is Arabic for 'crazy woman', and is used here in reference to Qays, the madman of the old Bedouin love story, Majnun Layla.

romance in action #17 *aka* we need to talk about the dominance of desire

Noah is a reference to the movie *The Notebook*, which glorifies manipulation and attention seeking as a form of romance.

The white light of Alma refers to the poem 'The Psychic' by Victoria Redel.

it's only called a 'revolution' when we feel proud of what happened today *aka* worry when they start to call it 'the situation'

Thawra is Arabic for 'revolution'.

Hala hala hala ho was the start of a popular chant in the Lebanese uprising.

Martyr's Square is a public square in downtown Beirut.

can there be such a thing as extreme tenderness?

A candle is consuming itself with desire refers to the version of *Layla and Majnun* written by Nizami.

the cartesian body: a coupling

This poem is a coupling, a form invented by Karen McCarthy Woolf. I have taken lines from René Descartes' *Sixth Meditation: Of the Existence of Material Things, and of the Real Distinction Between the Mind and Body of Man*, a founding text of dualism, which was the philosophical justification for hundreds of years of moral, economic and ecological warfare.

The poem is inspired by books on early capitalism's colonisation of the body and land by academics including Silvia Federici.

dinner during the week of rage

Warak enab is a Middle Eastern dish of stuffed vine leaves.

Hamoud is Arabic for 'lemon'.

Snayniyeh is a Middle Eastern desert.

Ha mout is everyday Arabic for 'will die'.

Sahteyn is a blessing when eating, like the French 'bon appetit'.

how it tastes to arrive from very far away: a broken ghazal

Shankleeh is a type of cheese, usually served with fresh, chopped tomatoes and onion.

running etcetera

Teta is how we refer to our grandmas, like the British 'nana'.
Balcon is French for 'balcony'.

pulling myself together

Albe is everyday Arabic for 'my heart'.

what if our hearts rumbled like our stomachs do

Too much fire gives birth to nothing is a quote from the anime film *Nausicaä of the Valley of the Wind* by Hayao Miyazaki.

speaking out loud

عربي is Arabic for 'Arabic'.

I'm a shape-shifting bitch you don't know who you loving is a line from the Princess Nokia song 'Brujas'.

in batroun

Batroun is an ancient city in Lebanon.

questions for the front and back of time

The concept of a good ancestor was inspired by Layla F. Saad.

acknowledgements

First and foremost, I must roll out all the gratitude for my editor and friend, Joelle Taylor. For pushing me to be honest, for pushing me to be observant, for pushing me to push language, for pushing me into myself so far I came out the other side singing songs I didn't know I knew.

Most importantly for fiercely reminding me — as I found myself fumbling around in mud amid an apocalypse — that my hands were sowing seeds, that tomorrow might just harvest.

A profound thank you to Rewa Zeinati for mentoring the spoken word artist to a page poet; you saw the most disastrous version of this manuscript and smiled reassuringly, pointing me in the direction of craft.

To Ollie O'Neill for being my dyke-in-tandem and giving me the best feedback notes, mostly because we all need a tiny lesbian gassing us up along the way.

Safiya Kamaria Kinshasa, Alice Frecknall, Leung Rachel Ka Yin and Sarah Fletcher for embarking on this journey to publication together, sharing moodboards, advice, warmth and a starting place.

Safia Elhillo for helping me see the bigger picture and connect the dots.

To Dr Jason Hickel, my professor who sharpened my political mind and the language of my resistance.

Thank you to my parents for providing support and a safety net, even when you're unnerved of who I am becoming. To my two sisters, Alix and Rhiannon, for being tethered to my heart wherever I take it. To my niece Sienna Rae for being the best reason for my generation to change the world ahead of us.

Thank you Jen Jen and Son Son for patiently putting up with the deplorable nature of a writer entranced, particularly while locked

down with me during the final stages of this manuscript.
To the rest of our chosen family — Nina, Tanya, Claire, Layla and the gang — for being love.

Huge thank you to Arts Council England for funding my time to write this, you make it easier for heart and integrity to survive inside this capitalist pressure cooker.

Thank you to Out-Spoken Press for being a trusted set of comrades, and mostly for becoming a women's publishing house long enough for me to get a book out without having to compromise my economy of sisterhood.

liberation *aka* جسدي

in the centre of Jassadi
is a tiny figure swaying

this is how my mother dances
this is where she is free

Other titles by Out-Spoken Press

Seder • Adam Kammerling

54 Questions for the Man Who Sold a Shotgun to My Father
Joe Carrick-Varty

Lasagne • Wayne Holloway-Smith

Mutton Rolls • Arji Manuelpillai

Contains Mild Peril • Fran Lock

Epiphaneia • Richard Georges

Stage Invasion: Poetry & the Spoken Word Renaissance
Pete Bearder

Nascent • Vol 1: An Anthology

Ways of Coping • Ollie O'Neill

The Neighbourhood • Hannah Lowe

The Games • Harry Josephine Giles

Songs My Enemy Taught Me • Joelle Taylor

To Sweeten Bitter • Raymond Antrobus

Dogtooth • Fran Lock

How You Might Know Me • Sabrina Mahfouz

Heterogeneous, New & Selected Poems
Anthony Anaxagorou

Titanic • Bridget Minamore

Email: press@outspokenldn.com